EPHESUS

TABLE OF CONTENTS

Published and Distributed by

Merkez: Duru Basım Yayın Reklamcılık ve Gıda San. Tic. Ltd. Şti.
Ticarethane Sok. Tevfik Kuşoğlu İşhanı No. 41/6 Sultanahmet
İSTANBUL
Tel: (+90.212) 527 49 95 Fax: (+90.212) 527 95 30

Şube : Atatütk Mah.1029 Sok.No:5/A Selçuk İZMİR Tel:0549 351 51 03
www.durubasim.com.tr info@durubasim.com.tr

Author: M. Salahattin Erdemgil

Photoraphs: Duru basım / Sercan Alan • www.sercanalan.com

Printing: Aktif Matbaa ve Reklam Hiz.San.Tic.Ltd.Şti
Tel 0212 698 93 54 Fax 0212 696 09 54

ISBN 978-9944-767-62-0

EPHESUS

During the construction of the parking area around the Church of St. John, some funeral objects belonging to a Mycenean tomb dating back to 1400 B.C. were revealed. They represented the oldest vestiges of the history of Ephesus. For a long time, the Mycenean city had been searched for in vain, and it was deemed probable that the tomb was a vestige of a settlement of seamen who sailed to that area for trade. Nevertheless, the hope of finding the foundations of the Mycenean city, not on the fragile peninsula but rather on the top of the hill of Ayasuluk, had not been abandoned. In fact, in 1990, during excavations around the Church of St. John, and in the citadel in order to discover archaeological layers, some findings that were previously unknown and dated back to the pre-historical period were brought to light.

That discovery was as important as the statues of Artemis and the Artemision excavated in 1860, since those architectural fragments are dated back to 3000 B.C., the Hittite period. Considering that the name of the city of Apassa is referred in the Hittite archives and that the etymologists declare that "Apassa" and "Ephesus" have the same roots and particularities in characters, it can be assumed that the vestiges revealed could be those of the antique city of Apassa.

The works of the pre-historical period displayed in the Ephesus Museum include stone axes, obsidian bill-hooks and terra-cotta. Some of those findings, which are dated back to 5000 years B.C., were discovered in the tumulus of Çukuriçi Höyük, at a distance of 400 m to the Door of Magnesia, during drilling work which lasted almost two years. The neolithic settlement indicates the remarkable change in the geographical form of Ephesus. It is known that the sea filled what is known as the province of Selçuk today, and the valley of the Cayster River (Küçük Menderes) was deep inland. In that period, Çukuriçi was situated on the coast and the hill of Ayasuluk was a small island. During the course of the centuries the alluvium carried by the Cayster River and the Marnas silted in the area, and as a result the sea descended back untiltoday at 6 km from the site. Nevertheless, it is still too early to talk about the Prehistorical Period of Ephesus, but the objects found in Çukuriçi Höyük evidence that the vestiges found could be remnants of the antique city of Apassa.

According to Herodotus, Ephesus was founded by colonists coming from the West during the first millennium, and the legend goes as follows: "Kodros, king of Athens, consulted the oracle before declaring war to the neighboring cities. The oracle answered that "The armies of the king who will die the first will be the winners". Kodros was killed by his enemies and his troops won. Another time a quarrel broke out between his sons for the share of the kingdom. Androclos, one of Kodros' sons, dreaming of founding a new city consulted the oracle about its future location. The oracle predicted that "A boar and a fish will indicate to you the exact place". Androclos and his men went out to sea and at the end of a journey came upon an unknown land. While they were grilling fish they had caught, fire spread to the bushes from where an enormous boar appeared. Androclos chased it and killed it. Remembering the prediction of the oracle, he founded his city on that spot, which seems to be the little hill facing the theater of Ephesus". Excavations on that area have not yet given any positive results. Still, according to Herodotus, before the arrival of Androclos, the country was occupied by the Carians and the Lelegians who claimed to be the oldest settlers of Asia Minor.

In the 8th century B.C., the Cimmerians attacked Ephesus and destroyed part of the city and the temple of Artemis. During the excavations in the agora, at 5 or 6 m beneath the surface, traces of constructions dated between the 8th and the 5th centuries B.C. were found, which led to the supposition that it was the settlement destroyed by the Cimmerians.

The i6th century was the Golden Age of Ephesus. She was the highest in art and sciences among the Ionian cities. Antique poets like Collinos and Hipponax, and the philosopher Heracleus were born in Ephesus. Her fame spread in the antique world, and attracted also the attention of

Croesus, King of Lydia. When his troops arrived at the gates of Ephesus, they came across a simple rope blocking the passage in front of the Artemision. The people of Ephesus had such a belief in Artemis that they did not consider someone would dare challenge her. The Lydian army entered city without any difficulty. But Croesus did not destroy the city; on the contrary, he donated aid for construction of the Artemis Temple. Besides, he built the famous columns with relieves for the temple Columna Cealata. Now exhibited at the British Museum, one of these columns bear the inscription "Built by King Croesus". Lydians ruled the city by tyranny. Although Ephesus did not favor tyranny due to the high taxes charged, they were autonomous in their interior affairs and continued its development.

The excavations in the city, particularly around the Artemis Temple, revealed many golden coins, electrons and ivory offerings dated back to the Lidian era.

Meanwhile, Anatolia was faced with the threat of Persian armies from the east. Kyros, the Persian king, captured Croesus during a clash, and ordered to burn him according to the Persian tradition. As depicted in many urns from the time, Croesus sat on a throne in the middle of a stack of wood. Just when the heap was set to fire, Croesus shouted "Oh, Solon'". Kyros stopped the fire, and asked Croesus what he meant. Croesus told him: "During the prime of my land, I invited Solon the Athenian philosopher to my palace in Sardes. I showed him my treasures, and asked him if there was anyone happier than me. Solon said, 'I cannot know if you are happy or not until I see you die.' Now I am about to burn, and the philosopher is right.' Listening to the story, Kyros decided to forgive Croesus and made him his consultant.

In 546 B.C., Harpagos, the commander of Kyros, invaded all Ionia, starting from Phokaia (Foça), the endmost Ion city. Persians, just like in many other lands, left the Ionians free in their internal affairs and religion. The united Karia, Phamphilia and Ionia to establish the satrap of Ionia. The people of Ephesus paid tributes (taxes) to the Persians, and supplied the Per-

sian army with troops and ships when necessary. However, the merciless rule of Persian satraps was far worse than the tyrants, even worse during the reigns of Kambyses and Dareios. Therefore, the Ionian cities united and started the revolt of Ionia. The revolters came to Ephesus, and under their guidance, followed the valley of Kaystros, and arrived at Sardes in three days, where they burnt down reed houses. The fire also destroyed the Kybele Temple. The destruction of the Kybele Temple was later used as an excuse for burning ancient temples in Greece. That rebellion was ended by the victory of the Persians in front of the little island of Lade near Miletus and the defeat of the Greek fleet which was allied with the Ionians. That time the Persians regained one by one the rebellious cities and destroyed them by pillage and fire.

Alexander the Great, King of Macedonia after having gathered certain troops of his Macedonian army reinforced by Greeks, crossed to Asia Minor to deliver it from the Achemidite yoke. In 334 B.C., he crossed the Hellespontand, and defeated the Persian troops allied to the Satrap of Ionia, Spithridates, on the banks of the Granicus (Bigaçay). Arrianos, Alexander's historian, called that battle "The Battle of the Horsemen". He tells us that at the very moment when Spithridates was going to hit Alexander the Great with his sword, he was killed by a Macedonian soldier. After that victory, Alexander the Great marched to Sardes and four days later entered Ephesus which

surrendered without resisting. According to Strabo, Greek geographer and historian, Alexander the Great offered freedom to the population of Ephesus. Being born the same night when the crazy Herostates set fire to the temple of Artemis, he wanted to participate in the reconstruction of the new Artemision but the Ephesians refused politely on the ground that a god (the Ephesians considered him as a demigod) could not present offerings to another god.

After Alexander the Great's death, Ephesus passed through a dark period during which his lieutenants succeeded each other, and it was only in 287 B.C. that the city regained her independence under Lysimacus, also one of Alexander the Great's lieutenants. Lysimacus had married in 299 B.C. To Arsinoe, daughter of Ptolemy, who was the first Pharaoh of Egypt. Between Mt Pion and Mt Coressus, he rebuilt the city following the typical planning of the Hellenistic period with streets cutting at right angles (Hippodamus) and surrounded by strong walls. Though he called that city Arsinae after his wife's name, the population did not keep it. Lysimacus ordered the population to move from the old city laid around the Artemision to the new one but that migration met a certain resistance. To overcome that resistance, he blocked the canalizations, thus obliging the inhabitants to move to the new city.

Arsinae was an ambitious woman who feared that Agothocles, the son of Lysimacus' first wife, would became his father's

successor instead of her son. She managed to make her husband believe that his son wanted to kill him. Lysimacus believed that lie and had his own son killed. Fearing for their lives, his first wife and some officers took shelter near the Seleucid empire, which they incited against Lysimacus. Therefore the Seleucids attacked Lysimacus' territory and the two armies met in the plain of Pedion where Lysimacus was killed. Then all his kingdom passed into the hands of the Seleucids in 281 B.C.

Under the reign of Antiochos Theos, Ephesus passed into the hands of the Ptolemies of Egypt, and in 196 B.C., under Antiochos III, it was recovered by the Seleucids who lost it again in 188 after the Treaty of Apamea, which gave the administration of Ephesus to the King of Pergamum until 133 B.C. At that date, Rome, having inherited the Kingdom of Pergamum, occupied Ephesus.

The Romans united Pamphylia and Ionia in a province called it the "Roman province of Asia", and Ephesus was named the capital by the Emperor Augustus. That way, Ephesus became the most important metropolis and trading center of Asia Minor. She was one of the five cities with a permanent Roman governor resident. In 27 B.C., after reorganizing the province, governors were replaced by Consuls. In the Senate in Rome, Ephesus was, with the provinces of Africa, the largest province. The title of Consul of the province of Asia became the summit of a career of any senator, because during that period the title of Consul was granted after 5 to 10 years of service as a pro-Consul, which was later extended to 15 years. Thus, considering that the service time of Consuls was only one year, hundred of persons were assigned to that post, including the future emperors Antoninius the Pious and Pupienus.

In the first century A.D., all religions co-existed freely in Ephesus: all the god and goddesses of Asia Minor, Greece, Rome, Palestine and Egypt were venerated. At the time of the emergence of Christianity in Jerusalem in 37-42 A.D., the Apostles were expelled after Christ's death. In 53 A.D., St. Paul came to Ephesus and for three years converted people and founded a church. According to the Gospel of St. Paul, he was helped by a new convert Timothy who helped him to spread Christianity in Ephesus. The new religion created discontent among the silversmith artisans who were selling silver statues of Artemis for the temple and were suffering losses. Demetrios, one of the influential silversmiths, gathered with his colleagues hundreds of supporters in the theater in Ephesus to stir up a riot against Paul, claiming "Artemis is the sublime goddess of Ephesus". St. Paul was obliged to flee from the city. St. Luke who wrote "The Life of the Apostles" wrote that event took place between 37-42 but did not mention St. John, who was there at the time with Virgin Mnary, who was entrusted to him by Christ. After St. Paul was beheaded on the walls outside Rome, St. John became the head of the Church of Ephesus. It is on that point that he wrote his Gospel and died. He was buried on the southern slope of Mt Ayasuluk. In the 4th century a small chapel was built on his tomb, and in the 6th century a cathedral was erected in dedication to St. John.

For Christians, the fact that St. Paul, St. John and the Virgin Mary lived in Ephesus, add to the interest given to the site. The first church dedicated to Mary was built there, and it was in this church that the Third Ecumenical Council took place, which established the fundamental principles of Christianity.In the 4th century Ephesus started to decline because of the silting

Floor mosaics in the hillside houses.

of the harbor, and in spite of all efforts to drain it, trading slowed down. During the 8th and 9th centuries, because of the weakness of the Byzantine administration, Ephesus loss strength. She was invaded from the sea by pirates and on land by Arab incursions. To consolidate its defence, the length of the surrounding walls was reduced but that being insufficient, the acropolis of the Mt Ayasuluk was reinforced by ramparts such that it became a second fortress.

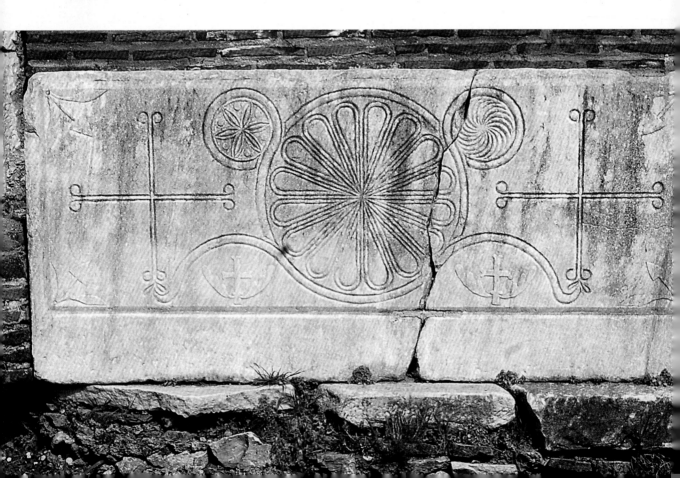

In 716, Arab troops led by the Caliph Suleyman spent the winter in Ephesus. In the 10th and 11th centuries, the city was abandoned and only a few ancient residents remained on the Mt Ayasuluk, called the Hagios Theologos.

When the first Turks arrived in Ephesus in 1304, the city had lost her old splendor and looked like an insignificant little town. She was incorporated in the Emirates of Aydinogullari who, inspired by Hagios Theologos, surrounded Mt Ayasuluk by walls. In the 16th century, the Arab traveller Ibn Batuta mentioned a city existing on the Western slope of the Mt Ayasuluk. Ayasuluk was effectively rebuilt a second time and decorated with mosques, baths, religious buildings and handsome monuments. For the Christians it had been for a time a bishopric. The Genovese and the Venetians establish there a trading center. The Turks built a naval dock and developed a new trade. However, the cultural and commercial life was surpassed by Izmir, and in the 19th century Ayasuluk became just a non-descriptive village. The railroad built in that period was used by the Turkish population which was displaced from Greece to the village of Sirince after the population exchange of the 20s. Thanks to the newly discovered interest in Ephesus, which give a boom to the tourism, Ayasuluk was renamed as Selçuk, and became a sub-prefecture in full expansion.

State Agora and surrounding edifices.

MONUMENTS SITUATED AROUND THE STATE AGORA

Entering on the site by the road leading to the House of Mary, the first ruins are the Baths of Varius. The excavations have not brought the whole edifice to light. Like in all typical Roman baths, one can distinguish the rooms of the frigidarium (cold room) and the calderium (hot room). The walls are made of large limestone blocks surmounted by vaults of bricks. The latrines and the palestra are on the southern side. The palestra, paved with mosaics, was covered to protect it from the weather. An inscription states that the Emperor Flavius and his wife built a hall on this site.

The large courtyard in front of the baths of Varius represents the State Agora of Ephesus. Built on a square plan, the northern side presented the Odeon and the Basilica, the southern side the Prytanee, and a street stretches with borders by columns. As the ground slanted on the western side, a filled wall was erected to level the agora. In front of the wall, there was a gallery of rooms for different purposes on two floors. The upper rooms would open on the courtyard and the downstairs directly on the agora.

In the middle of the agora was a small temple,

Remains of Water Palace in the State Agora.

Government Agora

Temple of Domitian.

Monument of Memmius.

Commercial Agora

Fountain of Trajan.

Temple of Hadrian.

Library of Celsus.

Grand Theatre

Harbour Street.

The Temple of Artemis

directed east-west and dedicated to the Egyptian goddess Isis, as it was the tradition of that period, because the hope of a second life in the other world was also a belief adopted by other cities in Asia Minor. In Ephesus, the second temple dedicated to an Egyptian goddess is the Temple of Serapis situated near the commercial agora. When the temple of Isis was destroyed under the reign of the Emperor Auguste, it was replaced with a group of the statues called the "Polypheme" which decorated its pediment on the facade of the Fountain Pollio on the side of the Square of Domitian. It is believed that the Emperor Auguste had that temple destroyed to show his antipathy towards the Egyptian after the affair between Antony and Cleopatra.

◁ *Remains of the Varius Bath.*

Odeon.

THE ODEON (BOULETERION)

It is situated near the baths and has the shape of a theater, which is why it is also called "the Little Theater". Build in the 1st century A.D., it was an auditorium and served as a meeting place for the members of the Senate but also as a concert hall. The city was administrated by two Councils: the Council Chamber (boule) and the Popular Chamber (Demos). The Council Hall had few members and held only a few meetings, once a year. The Popular Hall consisted of all the citizens of Ephesus to discuss daily problems.

Backing on Mt Pion, the Odeon presents a cavea divided by a diazoma. The members of the Council or the spectator entered by the parados through the stairs leading to the cavea. The stage building had two levels and five doors, the middle one being the largest and with a narrow podium on the proscenium.

THE PRYTANEION

Under the Roman Empire, Ephesus kept her administrative autonomy. The prytane, men or women were high servants who had a responsibility either concerning the cult or the administration. In the Prytaneion was the perpetual fire, a flame which burned night and day symbolizing every Ephesian's hearth represented by Hestia, goddess of the Family. The prytanes kept the fire alight, and had control over and the cults premises, the ceremonies, including the ritual of the offerings. They were chosen from the members of the noble and rich families and assumed

Vicinity of the State Altar.

Vicinity of the State Altar.

Statue of Artemisia.

Prytaneion.

their own expenses. However, they had no function concerning the Artemision.

Situated near the Odeon, this imposing edifice of high and massive columns had the form of a temple with a courtyard with a stoa in the front and a vast hall in the back.

The facade was ornamented by 8 doric columns on which were the names of the priests belonging to the Brotherhood of the Curetes, who were in the past linked with the cult of Artemis in the Artemision until the reign of Augustus who attached it to the Prytaneion.

In the center of the hall where the perpetual fire was burned, the hearth is still visible. Beside it were the statues of Artemis carefully buried, which are today exhibited in the Ephesus Museum. As it was done during the paleo-Christian period, all pagan statues were destroyed and for that reason it seems that the Artemis statues were buried by devout people to avoid their destruction.

Between the odeon, the prytaneion and the agora stretches a large construction on the basilical plan which seems to have been the Bourse and then was

transformed into a basilica. It is made of three naves surrounded by an Ionic colonnade decorated of bucranes (head of bull). The statues of the Emperor August and his wife Livia, as well as part of the impediment decorated with crosses exposed in the Ephesus Museum were found in the eastern part of the basilica.

Prytaneion and Domitian Square.

THE DOMITIAN SQUARE

The Domitian square is reached after the agora by a slight ascent where, set on a terrace, stands the Domitian temple that gives the name to the square. The western part has not been excavated but on the eastern side vestiges of most of the edifices have two storeys, the upper one overlooking the agora, which have been excavated. It is said that the first three edifices served as a hospital, but nothing has been revealed to support that hypothesis. On the other hand during the restoration of the Pollio fountain, the front of the pool was formed as an apse, decorated with a group of statues called "Polypheme". The high structure serving as a support to the facade gives an idea of its magnificence. According to an inscription discovered during the excavations, the fountain was erected in honor of Sextilius Pollio in 97 A.D.

THE DOMITIAN TEMPLE

Situated on the eastern side of the terrace, at the foot of Mt Coressos a marble altar was erected in front of which stood the seven-meter statue of the Emperor Domitian on a pedestal. The head of that statue was found as well as its left arm, both of which are exhibited in the Ephesus Museum; That statue was visible from every corner of the city. The terrace was surrounded by a sort of parapet decorated with columns and statues that brought a spectacular effect to the Domitian temple.

During the Roman empire, it was a great privilege for a city to be the guardian or to have a temple dedicated to an emperor (Neocore). Ephesus had that honor a

Temple of Domitian.

bit late with the temple dedicated to the Emperor Domitian (81-96 A.D.). He was assassinated in Rome by one of his servants and was declared "cursed" to the point that his name was erased from many monuments. Fearing the loss of the privilege of being "neocore", and faced with its rivals Izmir and Pergamum, the temple was rededicated to his father, the Emperor Vespasian.

THE MONUMENTAL GATEWAY OF MEMNIUS

That monumental cubical gateway standing on a podium of 4 steps is situated in the corner of the Domitian

Monument of Memmius.

square. Only part of it has been restored, because the upper part brought controversy. The four sides were linked to each other with arches in which were niches decorated of stele in relief hold by caryatides. A part of the steles has not survived until present. Actually the soldiers represented dressed in togas are Memnius, his father Caius and his grand father the dictator Sylla. In the beginning of the 4th century, the eastern facade was transformed into a fountain with basin and columns.

THE CURETES STREET

The Sacred Way starting from the Magnesian Gateway went around Mt Pion, and crossed the city to come back the Magnesian Gateway. The section between the Domitian Square and the Celsius Library was called the Curetes Street. The Curetes, a religious

Nike relief.

brotherhood, were serving the Artemision and once a year had a procession from the Prytaneion to reach Ortygie (Arvalya) near Kusadasi, to celebrate in a dramatic way the birth of the goddess Artemis. According to the legend, when Leto gave birth to her twins Artemis and Apollo, Zeus made terrible noises to distract Hera and avoid a fit of her jealousy.

Ephesus was rebuilt by Lysimacus following the plan of a Hippodamus, streets cut at right angles on a large artery, which did not correspond to the outline of the Sacred Way, but for that street he kept the original line. The Curetes Street was bordered by a stoa covered by a wooden roof under which existed houses and shops. The pavement of the sidewalks was made of mosaic, and the street itself was reserved for horses and carts. Many of the pedestals of statues of citizens and notables of the city bear honorific inscriptions. At the entrance of the street one can see, for example, the statue of a doctor called Alexandros. The traces of the wheels which are visible on the Sacred Way are not noticeable in the Curetes Street; besides, there is a difference of workmanship and material. Probably that is because the sober style used until the Roman era was contrary to their architectural style. The strong earthquakes which took place in 355, 358 and 368 were disastrous for Ephesus: each time statues collapsed, and marble slabs of the sidewalks were disjointed. After the two first earthquakes, the city was rebuilt with great effort, but

Curettes Road and Temple of Hadrian.

Fountain of Trajan.

TRAJAN ÇESMESI   TRAJ
I.S. 102 /114   10
Tib.Cl. Aristion
tarafından Imparator   der
Trajan'a ithaf edilen yapı   ro

38
Fountain of Trajan, dedicated by A

at the end of the v4th century, because of the silting of the harbor, Ephesus lost her economical strength, and after the third earthquake the columns which remained intact were used in other parts of the city or lifted up back to diminish the expenses of reconstruction. The sidewalks were renewed as well as the road, nevertheless the traffic was less intense, and the traces of the Roman chariots less visible. The axle of the Roman chariot wheels was of 110 cm, the depth of the track reached 10 cm, which lead to the conclusion that the chariots drove on the road as easily as trains on the railway. The Sacred Way, which has not been restored, shows distinctly these deep tracks.

THE TRAJAN FOUNTAIN (THE NYMPHEUM)

The fountain is situated on the right side of Curetes Street. To help to get a clearer idea of the original, a smaller model of the nymphea has been rebuilt which, according to the inscription of the architrave, certifies that it was dedicated to the Emperor Trojan (97-117 A.D.). The two pools were included in between the 3 sides (forming a U) on a two-storey monumental facade ornamented with pillars between which stood the statues of Dionysus, of a satyr, of Aphrodite and members of the imperial family. These statues were found here and are exhibited in the Ephesus Museum in the Fountains Hall.

THE SCHOLASTIKIA BATHS

These are situated near the Fountain of Trajan. The baths have 2 entrances: one on the main street, and the second one by a street parallel to the first. In 400 A.D. there were restored by a rich woman called Christiane Scholastikia, hence their name. The statue standing in the frigidarium is hers. This three-storey edifice is a pure example of Roman baths. The frigidarium holds in its center a

Statue of Scolastica.

Toilets.

Scolastica Bath.

vast elliptical pool of cold water because, following the tradition, it was the custom to refresh oneself by a cold dip before leaving the baths. The tepidarium (warm room) was a large vaulted room where it is still possible to see the marks of the supplying hot air pipes which run under the floor and the walls. At the bottom of the wall E, one can notice a piece of mosaic polychrome which covered the floor. The caldarium (hot room) has kept its original height and on the damaged floor one can see round prints left by marble blocks which positioned the place of the hypocaustes that warmed the room.

The used water ran into the canalization of the near by latrines. The latrines consisted of a rank of seats without any sepa-ration. In the center of the room stood a large pool.

THE HADRIAN TEMPLE

When the Emperor Hadrian (117-138) came to Ephesus in 128 A.D., he gave back to the city its title of "neocore" it had received when the temple of Zeus-Olympus was dedicated to the Emperor Domitian and was lost after his death. To regain that honor, the Ephesians built a large temple to the east of the city, near the city walls and called it Olympeion. During the Byzantine period, the marble was used as limestone and actually there is nothing left but the basement and capitals of the columns which were 2 meters high.

The Hadrian Temple situated on Curetes street bears on the architrave an inscription dedicated to the Emperor Hadrian by P. Quintillus. The facade is ornamented by a four-columned portico with square columns on the sides. The portico is surmounted by a magnificent pediment decorated with classical motifs and in its center the head of Tyche, goddess of Fortune, who was the symbol of the city. The lintels of the central door bear a decoration in relief in patterns of eggs and pearls. The second pediment, with acanthus leaves, had in its center a bust of a naked woman looking like Medusa. On both sides of the door are friez-

Temple of Hadrian.

es illustrating Androclus killing a wild boar, the procession of Dionysus and the priest Curetes during the restoration. The original relieves are sheltered at the Ephesus Museum and are replaced by plaster casts.

In front of the temple, plinths bear the name of four emperors: Diocletian, Maximian, Constantine the Chlore and Galerius (293-305).

Next to the temple, near the Museum Administration, is a vaulted edifice which was, under the Roman rule, a spice market. During the Roman period, the spices brought from Asia Minor and Central Asia were exported by sea from the harbor of Ephesus. Spices were also very appreciated by the Ephesians.

THE SHOPS

The porticoes facing the Hadrian Temple sheltered shops on two storeys. Some on the upper floor had an exit in the back directly on the houses. The well-off citizens of the city would do their shopping in the shops of the agora and the adjacent streets. Those who had time would spent their afternoon in the baths.

It is known that trade was flourishing in Ephesus. All food was produced on the large farms of the province. On the other hand, all the well-protected trade routes of Anatolia lead to Ephesus. All sort of finished products could be found as well as a choice of material. Ephesus was linked by sea to all harbors of the Mediterranean, particularly to Rome and Egypt. Alexandria, the largest harbor of Egypt, was in close commercial relation with Ephesus. Spices, rice and glass objects as well as slaves were imported and spices, silk, metal, cloth of all sorts, as well as fresh and dry fruits were exported. The columns of pudding-stone found in the city came from Egypt. A cosmopolitan population came from far away countries to the city: merchants, sailors, Romans, rich landowners, soldiers, workers and slaves formed the human mosaic of the people living in Ephesus. The inhabitants lived in different sectionx of the city according to their social status. For example, the rich families were gathered on the Curetes

Temple of Hadrian.

Street and the Marble Road as well as in the center of the city, in wealthy houses, when the workers and the servants resided in the lower part of the city in uncomfortable lodgings. Under the reign of the Emperor August, Ephesus had a population of 200.000 people. In that period, under the influence of the Pax Romana, the ramparts lost their importance as a system of defence, and the city spread until the actual province of Selçuk.

THE HOUSE BLOCKS ON THE SLOPE

When Lysimacus rebuilt the new Ephesus, the plan foresaw residential quarters on each side of the Curetes Street, spread on the slopes in terraces cut by narrow streets, each terrace having two houses. The first excavation of that area, which is situated in front of the Hadrian temple, started in 1950, and was resumed in 1979. All frescoes and mosaics discovered during the first work are exhibited in the Ephesus Museum, while the last have been kept on the site. In 1986, two houses of this area, the houses A and B, were opened to the public.

The houses of that residential quarter are of the type with a peristyle, including an inner open yard around which the rooms were laid. They were very luxurious houses with a central heating system, similar to what we know today, supplied with cold and hot water, and decorated with frescoes and mosaic floors, wooden or bamboo furniture, bronze accessories, full length statues or busts in marble and precious metal. All were for common use, except for the clothes.

The houses were generally built on 3 floors: the ground floor consisted of a kitchen, a living room, a bathroom and rooms for the servants, aand the bedrooms were on the first floor. The ground floors are still in good condition, but nothing has remained of the upper floors. There is almost no windows except for a few examples, which explain the obscurity of the rooms, with light and air coming from the inner courtyard (impluvium).

Contrary to the Roman architecture of cult monuments with a facade richly decorated and an interior really modest, here the houses present an unadorned exterior but a comfortable and richly decorated interior. They are dated back to the first century B.C.; however, because of earthquakes and fires, they have been rebuilt or restored many times. The childish writings on

Hillside houses and shops on the street.

Images from hillside houses decorated with floor mosaics and frescoes.

the walls in general have given way to the renovation of the frescoes. In certain cases, 7 or 8 layers of paint have been noticed. The frescoes of the upper part of the wall are still visible but, those of the lower part can not be identified although modern techniques are employed.

HOUSE A

The house is accessed by a staircase situated in front of the Hadrian temple; the stairs, at the right of the entrance door lead to the upper floor, which is almost completely destroyed. Another staircase leads to the ground floor. As is found in all houses in Anatolia, there is a fountain near the entrance to permit the inhabitants to wash themselves

before entering the house. The impluvium is paved with marble, and decorated at each corner by columns with Doric capital who hold the beams of the upper floor. In the wall on the North, there is a fountain with double pools. Just behind it is the large living room which was converted in the 3rd century into 2 small rooms by a wall.

The room on the left side is

called the "Theater Room". The owner was probably a lover of the fine arts because the walls of this house, date back to the 2nd century A.D., are covered by frescoes illustrating theater scenes. The narrow wall to the right of the door presents a scene from a very well known comedy of Menander, painted on a red background with light brown designs showing two masked figures under the inscription of "sikynion". The left wall is also of red background and shows, as the inscription mentions, a scene from the Orestes of Euripides. Orestes is seen lying down, talking to his sister, Electra. The actors are masked in the Roman theatrical tradition. The large northern wall bears a vast fresco divided by Corinthian fluted columns. Each scene depicts naked characters. The upper part represents a mythological scene: Acheloos and Herakles fight in the witness of a group of persons, including Acheloos, Herakles, a man and a woman and next to them, and two men, one of them naked.

According to the legend the River God Acheloos wished to marry Dejanire, the daughter of the king of Calydon, but she

preferred Herakles, fearing the ability of Acheloos to change himself into a bull or a dragon. Under those metamorphoses, Acheloos attacked Herakles but he was defeated. It is that legend which is the theme of the decoration of the wall.

The function of the two small dark rooms with walls decorated by floral frescoes opening on the large room is not known.

A door opening on the vestibule leads to the bath room and the heating room. On the wall, marks of pipes for the heating system can be noticed as well as a little service door.

THE HOUSE B

It is the house by the vestibule of House A. It has the usual characteristics of classical Roman houses, but it is larger and fancier. According to the results of the excavations it was inhabited until the 6th century and passed through many restorations during the centuries without losing the elements of its decoration.

The first large room shows frescoes taken from the theme of the muses, which is why it is called the "The Room of the Muses". Unfortunately those frescoes suffered many fires and are in a poor condition. Only the eastern wall has preserved a panel, on which is Thalia, the Muse of Comedy.

Built in the peristyle, this house is larger than the other, showing a beautiful pavement of geometrical black, yellow and white mosaic designs. The impluvium is still in good shape. Originally, it was surrounded by 8 columns, but during the Byzantine period, a new column was added to the southern side and were linked by brick vaults. In the middle of the yard was a fountain and a well used in times of lack of water. The exterior walls of that inner yard were covered by marble slabs and indicated the wealth of the owner.

In the south-west corner, where steps lead to the upper floor, one can see the most beautiful piece of art of the house: a splendid panel of mosaic polychrom illustrating the abduction of amphitrite by Triton, who is seating her up on a sea horse. The vaulted niche next to it was the "tablinium": a room in which the owner had his siesta. The vault is covered with a glass mosaic which is one of the finest examples of the art from the Roman period. It represents Eden with fruits, flowers and roosters as well as peacocks and panthers held in leash by Eros. Right in the center are the busts of Dionysus and Ariadne framed in a

double red circle. This mosaic suffered a lot of damage during the excavations, but after a long and patient work, the experts were able to reconstruct and put it back to its original place.

It is in that peristyle house a statue of Artemis, a bust of a prince, a marble basket and a bronze foot of a table, which are now part of the beautiful artefacts exhibited in the Ephesus Museum, were revealed.

On the western wall of the yard, a door leads to the kitchen, with a hearth still in good condition. Here -found a sort of a marble jar was found with pipes of different sizes functioning as a water divider. The flow of the water was distributed according to the need of each room and each pipe had a cork that is used to open and close the running of the water. The kitchen is paved with mosaic and the frescoes with similar the motifs to those in the inner yard walls.

On the northern side of the

house there are 2 rooms, the eastern one being the triclinium, the dining room of the Roman houses. Here the Romans received their honorable guests. It was composed of 3 kline (couches) on which people would eat and drink in a reclining position. On each side of the entrance, placed in a niche, is a marble covered wash-basin with two taps for cold and warm water. The niche of semi-apsidal form is adorned with a beautiful polychrome glass mosaic work. The niche of the western side is decorated by a scene of a woman surrounded by 2 swans, which is probably the figure of Aphrodite. The eastern niche, which is more deteriorated, shows a man's face. The other room is the family dining room which has a large marble bench with an impression of a bar counter outside.

On the western side of the peristyle, there was a door leading to a second inner yard to acess the side street, which was

Details from hillside houses.

later surrounded by walls. The yard is paved with marble, and has four thick columns. In a corner, one can notice the 3 latrines which look very much like the ones used today. The walls are decorated by frescoes representing Africans slaves and some inscriptions concerning those personages.

SQUARE

There is a little square on Curetes street, facing the Celsius Library on which stands, to the right, the brothel and to the left a fountain dating back to the Byzantine era, and the Gate of Hadrian, which was built on two storied columns with three vaulted entrances, is the starting point of the road leading to Ortygie. The restoration work has not been finished yet. The street stretching to the north is the Marble Road, still in good condition except for the portico standing on the right side which was destroyed to be replaced by later buildings. On the other side, stood the Stoa of Nero built at 2 meters above the level of the Marble Road. It was a covered portico with columns on each side, above the nearby commercial agora.

Along the Marble Road, one can notice the visible marks of the damage done during the Byzantine period by pulling out iron and lead bars that hold the large marble blocks of the pavement and the plinths for the statues. The left side was limited by different levels done by raftered marble slabs with a metallic border which is described as an indication towards the brothel in guides. This "sign board" represents a woman's head surrounded by lines in between which are patterns of hearts and the print of a left foot, which would have meant "A little bit on the left, there are beautiful women, who in spite of their broken heart would give you love".

That public house (Paidiskeion), whose upper storeys have collapsed, is a house of the

Gate of Hadrian.

Footprint on the Marble Road.

peristyle type with two entrance doors: one giving on Curetes Street and the other in the Marble Road. It şs named after the statue of the god Priapus which was revealed here (in the Ephesus Museum). The large room on the western side, paved with a mosaic symbolizing Four Seasons, was the dining room and an adjacent bath room with an elliptical basin in the west corner with mosaic floors representing 3 women eating and drinking, a standing servant and a mouse nibbling crumbs on the ground and a cat. The house was built between 98-117 under the reign of Trajan.

THE CELSIUS LIBRARY

This is the restored edifice located on the western side of the square. It was built as the tomb of Tiberius Celsius Polemanus, Proconsul of the Province of Asia. The funeral chamber, under the central niche, contains a sculpted marble sarcophagus. The building itself, on two floors separated by a wooden balcony, was used as a library where manuscripts and rolls of parchments placed in the niches were kept. To protect the manuscripts from humidity, a passage was built in the masonry to permit air circulation, behind the niches. The funeral chamber can be accessed by a passage on the right.

The two-storey facade reflects all the architectural characteristics of the period of the Emperor Hadrian. The building was placed on a podium formed by large steps leading to the first floor. It was decorated with Corinthians columns, behind which are 3 doors, the middle one being the biggest and the highest, framed by classical motifs with decorated lintels. Between the doors, in the niches, are the statues symbolizing Wisdom, Fortune, Science and Virtue, which were, as can be read on the inscription of the pediment, the virtues of Celsius. The original statues are in the Ephesus Museum in Vienna. On the upper floor the columns are shorter and hold triangular or half spherical pediments with windows.

As the library was built after the Southern Gate of the agora and the Great Altar, space was limited, and to compensate it and to give the library the monumental perspective worthy of it, a trick was used. The podium on which the building stands has the form of an arch, which means that the center is slightly higher than the angles. The capitals of the columns rising on the angles have been a bit shortened to give the illusion of depth and to

Sophia.

Sophia.

Ennoia.

achieve a stately aspect.

The Celsius Library was built by his son, Tiberius Julius Aquila. However he died before it was finished and his heirs saw the completion of the monument. Tiberius left 25.000 dinars for the purchase of manuscripts by will.

In 262 A.D., during the Goths invasion, the Celsius Library was set on fire, but the facade was rescued. Like the other Ephesus edifices, in the 6th century, the Library went through a restoration but, a violent earthquake destroyed it again. Between 1972 and 1978, the Austrian F.Hueber, an archaeologist specialist in restoration, completed the work on the facade.

Episteme.

Library of Celsus at night.

Gate of Mazeus and Mithridates.

THE COMMERCIAL AGORA AND THE SOUTHERN DOOR OR MAZEUS AND MITHRIDATES GATE

The monumental Gate of Ephesus commercial agora nearby the Celsius Library is situated on the southern side. Like every monument dedicated to victory, it has 3 passages. The arches are covered by black marble slabs, and the others with white marble. The main passage is slightly behind the two others, giving an impression of depth that cut the monotony. The borders of the pediment are indented and give the effect of a crown. The inscription engraved on the bronze wall of the pediment reads in Lati: "That gate, built by Mazeus and Mithridates and the people, is dedicated to the Emperor Augustus, the great Pontiff, son of Caesar, 12 times Consul, 6 times Tribune and to his wife Livia; dedicated also to the Emperor Marcus Agrippa, father of Lucius, 3 times Consul, 6 times tribune and to Julia, daughter of Augustus."

Mazeus and Mithridates were two slaves at the service of the Emperor August. After being freed, they built that door to prove their devotion to the imperial family.Other than that door, there existed 2 others which have not yet been restored.

The agora occupied a quadrilateral of 111 meters on the sideways. Built in the 3rd century B.C., it was restored under the reign of the Emperor Caracalla (211-217 A.D.). According to the results of the excavations, it appears that the Sacred Way would pass at the eastern angle and that on each side there were 2 terra cotta sarcophaguses from the city of Clazomenes but on the western angle, at an inferior level, houses were found dated back to the 6th or 7th century.

The agora was surrounded

by porticoes sheltering shops, except on the north side. It was a large commercial center. Inscriptions of laws and prices of products sold in the agora have been brought to the surface. The porticoes supported by granite columns were covered by a wooden roof, protecting in that way the passer-bys the from the sun in summer and from the rain in winter.

At the extremity of the south portico, a stairway leads to the Temple of Serapis. Built as a prostyle, the columns were made of a single marble block weighting many tons. The door of the cult room, made of two large open gates, was so heavy that to facilitate its opening it was set on wheels, whose marks can be seen on the stylobate. The fragments, spread next to the temple leads to the assumption that it was never finished.

During the course of its history, Ephesus carried on excellent commercial and social relations with Egypt. The Ephesus Museum exhibits a large marble block engraved with a commercial treaty between Ephesus and Alexandria on which is the figure the Egyptian goddess Serapis and Artemis from Ephesus. The temple iis dated back to the 2nd century.

Grand Theatre and

Grand Theatre and Harbour Street.

THE GREAT THEATER

With its seating capacity of nearly 24.000, it is the largest theater of Asia Minor. Built on the slope of Mt Pion, facing the Arkadian Way and the Marble Road that linked the theater to the harbor, it has a majestic appearance. As the harbor was the entrance of the city, the first construction seen by travellers coming from the sea was the theater. Its attractiveness and rich appearance aimed to surprise and impress the visitors.

The building of the scene, standing between the Arkadian Way and the Marble Road, had 3 storeys and reached 18 meters. The wall behind the orchestra was richly decorated with columns, relieves and niches with triangular pediments which contained statues. During the excavations, all the architectural fragments in front of the theater were collected to be used for the restoration.

The first two storeys are in relatively good condition. On the ground floor, a long corridor, the postcenium, leads to the actors and choristers rooms, and had in the middle a door for access to the orchestra. On the first floor, the stage, where the acting took place, was set on a podium forming a hemicycle of 2.50 meters high. On each side were two corridors (parados) where the choristers stood, but also allowed the actors to come closer to the orchestra to talk with the spectators. The importance of those parados diminished during the many modifications of the theater.

The cavea, divided in 3 maeniana by 2 diazoma, was surmounted by a columned portico on its upper part. The first rows, reserved for the high ranking citizens of the city, had marble backs. Between the cavea and the orchestra, an imperial box stood on a podium. The stairs dividing the cavea permitted the movement of the spectators and easy access to their seats.

The first theater dated probably back to the Hellenistic Period and was rebuilt by the Emperor Claudius (31-42). The building took 70 years to complete due to modifications necessary at that time. When the Apostle St. Paul visited Ephesus, the work on the theater was not yet completed.

Actors were all males wearing masks as it is shown on the frescoes of the residential houses in that area. The entrance to the theater had an admission fee.

THE MONUMENTS OF THE ARKADIANE WAY

The large artery between the harbor and the theater was called the "Arkadiane Way" in honor of the Emperor Arcadius (395-408) who restored it. An inscription discovered between ruins certifies that the way was lit at nights by lanterns, which was very unusual during antiquity, and only Rome, Ephesus and Antioch had that privilege. During the Byzantine Period, the center of the way was marked by four large columns on which stood statues of the Four Apostles. Only one of them has survived until present. Each extremity on the Way had a monumental door, which is in ruins today.

At the corner of the theater, one can see the vestiges of a gymnasium dating back to the first century. A section of the wrestling school has been under excavations but has not been completely revealed yet. It was a very important monument in Ephesus whose facade bordered the Sacred Way and the Arkadiane Way. The wrestling school, surrounded by columns, has on the northern side a tribune for the spectators to watch the competitions. The track is on the northern side of the Arkadiane Way.

Further ahead, is a vast square 200 m long, the Veru-

Harbour Street.

lanus Square, which has not been excavated yet. Nearby, the remains of a gymnasium have been brought to light and the Harbor Baths were the drilling has not yet been finished.

THE CHURCH Occ xF HAGHIA MARIA

Turning to the right of the Arkadiane Way is the entrance booth to visit the church which was the first dedicated to Virgin Mary and where the Ecumenical Council took place in 431. It was built on the site of a sanctuary for the Muses in the 2nd century. According to an inscription found, the old sanctuary served as a medical school and that doctors and professors who practiced there had the privilege of exemption from customs tax. During that time, travellers had to pay a heavy tax to have the right to travel between the cities of a province, and the exemption given to the doctors of that sanctuary demonstrate the importance they were granted.

The church is an edifice of basilica design with three naves to which an apse was added in the chief nave which transformed the basilica in a church in the 4th century. On the western side, the building was preceded by a vast atrium with columned porticoes, a pavement of marble slabs, and a baptistery. The chief nave, narrower than the lateral naves, was separated by a row of columns linked to each other by a barrier. The ground was paved with mosaics, which have disappeared. Some examples of the mosaics can be seen in the narthex. At the end of the 5th century, the church was in such a poor condition that the Emperor Justinian (527-565) built, right in the middle, a second smaller church with a dome and added small chambers to the sides of the new apse. The large marble ompholos in the church originates from the Harbor Baths.

The Ecumenical Council of 431, which took place in that church, concerned the controversy provoked by the bishop of Antakya, Nestorius, on the understanding of the person

Church of Mary, Baptismal Tank and Apses.

House of Virgin Mary.

of Christ, denouncing the Divine Motherhood of the Virgin Mary, arguing that the fact was not mentioned in the writings of the Apostles. The Emperor Theodosius, disturbed by the heresy, decided to call a council in Ephesus to which the Bishop of Constantinople Nestorius, the Bishop of Alexandria Cyril, the Bishops of Ephesus and Antakya as well as a delegate of the Pope participated. The city passed through a rough time during the council, but in the official reports, the fact that the Virgin Mary had come to Ephesus was recognized.

THE STADIUM AND THE VEDIUS GYMNASIUM

With a length of 230 meters and a width of 30 meters, the stadium was shaped like a "horse shoe". It was the center of boxing competitions, wrestling and running. On the western side was a monumental portico with three vaulted gates and a double row of columns. Built on the slope of Mt Pion, the rows of the steps were directly cut from the rock. As for its other part, on the northern side, it rests on a strong infrastructure. The first stadium dates back to the Hellenistic Period and was rebuilt under the reign of Nero (54-68). The restoration work is still in process.

In the 3rd and the 4th century, the circus games (gladiators' fights and wild animals) were very popular in most of the Roman Empire. On the contrary, except for Pergame, those shows were not appreciated in the Province of Asia. There are no arenas in the cities of Asia Minor. For some occasions, the extremity of the stadium would simply be closed by a fence to change it in an arena. In Ephesus, there were some families of gladiators like the Vedius, who created a school. It is known that many Christians were thrown to the wild beasts, so, when Christianity became the state religion,

Cave of Seven Sleepers.

and as a retaliation, stadiums and temples, such as the Temple of Artemis, were destroyed and the material recycled to be used in the construction of churches like the Church of St. John. For that reason, there are no rows of steps left in the stadium.

Excavations started in the stadium in 1992 brought to the surface a small chapel of a more recent period. It was discovered at the entrance of the vaulted gallery. The Sacred Way passed right in front of this gallery. It seems that the Coressos Gate stood in this area, but no excavations have been executed so far.

On the other side of the Sa-cred Way stands the Vedius Gymnasium, one of the great monuments of Ephesus. According to an found inscription, it was built by the famous gladiators' family Vedius and dedicated to the Emperor Antonin the Pious (138-161). The entrance on the east, was a monumental gate with columns, a sort of propyleum opening on a square palester. All the remains discovered during the excavations are exhibited in the Izmir Museum.

THE GROTTO OF THE SEVEN SLEEPERS

It is situated at the foot of Mt Pion, accessible by the Magnesian Gate and the Vedius Gymnasium. Grottoes, like the grotto of the Seven Sleepers on the slope of Mt Pion are the results of tectonic movements. In this grotto was a small chapel surrounded by many tombs. During the archaeological excavations in 1927-28, when the chapel was cleared, a real necropolis was discovered with hundreds of tombs dating back

Drawing of the Temple of Artemisia.

to the 5th and the 6th centuries. Some Christians claim that Mary Magdalene was buried there.

The main conflict between the first Christians and Rome was the fact that the later refused to follow the cult to the emperor and the sacrifices made on the altars of the temples. To oppose those customs was considered a crime, and the history of the grotto is associated with that fact. In 250 A.D., under the reign of the Emperor Decius, seven young Christians were persecuted for refusing to make the offering to the temple, took shelter in the grotto and fell asleep. When they went out to get some food, they realize that they had not been asleep one night but 200 years

(the Muslims say 309 years) and they learned that Christianity had become a state religion. The Emperor Theodosius II accepted that resurrection as a miracle from God and when they died, they were buried in that grotto in which a small chapel was built.

THE ARTEMIS TEMPLE

The first excavations were launched in 1863, led by the archaeologist J.T. Wood for the British Museum, in order to discover one of the Seven Wonders of the World: the Artemis Temple. First of all he mistook the Baths of the Harbor

whose ruins were near the surface for being the bases of the Artemision, but later he understood his error when he found the real position of the temple, from where he carried on his work.

In 1869, during the campaign of excavations in the theater, he found an inscription that certified that the cult objects, lent by the temple for religious ceremonies, were brought to the city through the Sacred Way to the Magnesian Gate, to be brought back to the Artemision by the same way. Drilling works starting from this gate led him finally to the site of the temple.

As early as 1895, systematic digs at the Artemision were

Remains of the Temple of Artemisia in Ayasuluk, İsa Bey Mosque and the Castle.

entrusted to the Austrian Archaeological Institute, and since 1965the archaeologist Dr. Anton Bammer has been the head of the excavations. During the last years, vestiges of an ancient temple, dated back to the Archaic Period, which was believed until now to be the time of its first construction, has been found.

According to Strabo, this sanctuary was built and destroyed seven times, and he claims that the Ancients considered it as one of the Seven Wonders. During antiquity, this temple stood near the sea but today its location is 5 km from the coast. The Cayster River and its alluvium have always created problems. The oldest traces of the existing temple are dated back to the 14th century B.C. There are Mycenean ceramic cups, which leads to the assumption that a sanctuary dedicated to Cybele existed earlier than the archaic temple dated back to the 7th century B.C., from which terra cottas with geometrical design, jewels and some ivory artefacts have been taken. Some capitals of the Ionic columns of that temple, probably destroyed by the Cimmerians, can be seen in the British Museum.

In 570 B.C., after the erection of the temple of Hera in Samos, the Ephesians decided to build a new temple and gave the responsibility of the work to architects from Crete, Chersiphron and his son Metagenes as well as the architect Theodore who had built the temple of Hera because of his experience and because the ground in Samos was marshy like Ephesus. Under the foundations he spread a layer of coal covered with leather.

This temple of dipteral design, 115,14 meters long and 55,10 meters wide, shows the knowledge of the Cretans on the Egyptian, Hittite and Assyrian architecture. It is the largest marble temple ever built. On the sides of the temple stood a double row of columns which were 19 meters high with a diameter of 1,21 m, which gave depth to the edifice. According to Pliny the Younger, the numbers of the columns was 127 but the number of columns on the facade have always been debated. Recent research suggest that the facade in front and in the back of the temple shows it had a double colonnade. Pliny the younger claims that the facade had 36 sculpted columns, but considering that he lived in the first century A.D., it is practically impossible that he saw the Archaic temple. He must have refer to ancient texts and as the Hellenistic temple was built on the Archaic, his description remains valid. The 36 sculpted columns called "columnae caelatae" were offered by Croesus king of Lydia, as is proven by the dedication placed on the drum of the column exhibited in London: "it is a present from Croesus" attesting also to the solicitude of that king for the Artemision. Herodotus also attests that inscription.

The blocks of the architrave which rested on columns weighing 24 tons. It is amazing how such heavy blocks were lifted to a height of 20 m with the techniques of the time. The altar which stood in front of the temple, destroyed by the Cimmerians, was rebuilt on a podium situated at the base to give the illusion of steps. During the excavations many ex-voto artefacts were found scattered in the area.

In 356 B.C., the Artemision was set on fire by a crazy man, Herostrate, the very night, it is said, of the birth of Alexander the Great. He may have wanted his name to be immortalized in history. With a new ardor, the Ephesians started the construction of a new temple which, by its magnificence, was to surpass the previous. When Alexander the Great arrived in Ephesus, the temple was not yet finished. The Hellenistic temple measured at that time 105 meters to 55 meters, and kept the same plan as the original. The columns of the facade were also sculpted like those of the Archaic temple Pliny the younger and Vitruvus claim that one was sculpted by the famous sculptor Scopas. Praxiteles also helped in the decoration of the altar.

One of the columns belonging to the Hellenistic temple, exhibited in the British Museum, represents the sacrifice of Alcestes who agreed to die to save her husband.

The Artemision had the advantage of many privileges, including the right of shelter, giving immunity to all who took refuge in the temple. Alexander the Great enlarged that limit to outside the temple. The King Mithridates pushed its limits to the distance where an arrow shot from the pediment would fall. The Emperor Marc Antony doubled the perimeter of the asylum area as Julius Caesar had done for the temple of Didyma.

İsa Bey Mosque, with the Castle in the background.

That privilege, which included a section of the city, resulted in a gathering of outlaws around the sanctuary.

The Artemision was administered by priests and the high priest called "Megabysos" was castrated. According to Strabo, he was specially chosen among the priests from Asia Minor origins. That position was an honorary title. Another strange custom of this sanctuary was that it functioned like a bank. The acceptance of gifts or valuable objects left as deposit, the opening of credit for the budget of the temple, were on the sole responsibility of the Megabysos.

THE CITADEL OF AYASULUK AND THE CHURCH OF ST. JOHN

During the Byzantine Period, the city took the name of Haghios Teologos. The Selcukians, drawing their inspiration from the name, called it Ayasuluk, and finally it became Selçuk in 1950. The citadel which was erected on the ancient acropolis, has been the object of excavations that brought to light, on the eastern slope, pre-historical vestiges of the Mycenean Period. Under the Romans it was mostly used as a necropolis, and the Byzantines surrounded it by a wall. That area has not been dug systematically. Inside the citadel, exist a chapel, a small mosque, baths and many cisterns. When the Turks arrived in the 8th century, they settled themselves there, restored the city wall and found a new city on the slope of the acropolis. The surrounding wall was fortified by many towers and two gates: one on the east, the other on the west.

The St. John Basilica standing on the south slope of the citadel, is among one of the most beautiful monuments of the Byzantine period. According to the historian Eusebe, the Apostles were chased out of Jerusalem in 37-42 and St. John to whom Jesus had entrusted his mother Mary, came to Ephesus with her where he wrote his Gospel and his last will. At his death, he was buried on the hill of Ayasuluk. In the 4th century, a modest little church was built on his grave which was replaced later by a sumptuous sanctuary erected by the Emperor Justinian (527-565) and his wife Theodora.

The cross-shaped basilica covered by six domes hold up by massive pillars, sheltered the tomb of St. John, placed just beneath the central dome. It had three naves formed by rows of columns covered by blue-veined marble which supported the capitals, with the monograms of the emperor and his wife, attesting to the exact date of its erection. These columns were linked by brick vaults which supported the first floor. The ground of the niche placed in front of the crypt was raised higher by two steps and its small dome was upheld by four spiral columns. The polychrome mosaics that covered the ground were pulled out one by one. Its pieces are still visible in some places, and give an idea of what the ground looked like. It was believed that the dust raised from the grave and gathering on the windows had a curative power and in the Middle Ages, the basilica became an important shrine for pilgrimages.

On the western side was the narthex and an exonarthex. Like every church, the entrance on western side was made by a handsome atrium whose different levels was applied by raising higher walls. The yard was surrounded by a covered portico with a gallery opening onto a parapet on the exterior. Under the western portico a large cistern with three pools was discovered, which served as a warehouse for the material during the building of the Isa Bey Mosque. Between the atrium of the basilica and Isa Bey Mosque, another church was discovered

Pursuit Gate, Church of St. John.

Model of the Church of St. John.

St. John. Church

Main interior of the Church of St. John and the grave of St. John before the apses.

and a building with many rooms, which could have been the residence of a bishop in the 5th century.

In the 7th century, to protect the basilica from the Arab incursions, it was surrounded by walls linked to the citadel on the north, giving the building the appearance of an interior fortress. In the 14th century, the Arab traveller Ibn Batutah visited Ephesus and mentioned that the basilica was used as a mosque. After the construction of the Isa Bey Mosque, the basilica lost its importance and collapsed during an earthquake at the end of the 14th century. The Gate of the Persecution, which formed the entrance of the fortified city on the south, was preceded by a small yard guarded by two high towers. That gate was ornamented by a sculpted frieze representing Achilles, which was taken to England by the English archaeologists and placed in the Voburn Abbey.

The first excavations of the basilica were carried out in 1921-22 by the archaeologist Sotiriu. Then the work was entrusted to the Austrian Institute of Archaeology which brought to light the second floor columns of the basilica nave. Since 1976, the administration of the Ephesus Museum has continued the excavations and the restoration, which allowed the creation of a very sightly archaeological park around and in the basilica, appreciated by all visitors.

HOUSE OF VIRGIN MARY

Christ entrusted his mother, Virgin Mary, to St. John, who was his friend and apostle. When being crucified in Golgota, Christ saw that his mother and his favorite disciple was with him, called to his mother: "Oh woman, there is your son!" Then he said to his apostle: "There is your mother!" After that moment, St. John never left Virgin Mary. After the ascension of Christ, Virgin Mary met with the apostles and friends of Christ in Jerusalem and built the first church.

St. John was one of the leading founders of Christianity. He is the "favorite disciple of the Messiah" and the one to whom Christ entrusted his mother. During these years, when Christianity was spreading, the first Christians were tortured in Jerusalem. St. John's brother was also assassinated. After the violence and oppression aggravated, the apostles left the country. St. John helped Virgin Mary to flee from this environment of mistrust, and brought her to Ephesus, which was one of the most important cities of the time. Considering the information in holy scripts, it is highly probable that Virgin Mary and St. John arrived in Ephesus around 42 A.D. St. John continued his works to spread Christianity after migrating, and managed the first Christian community in Ephesus. He lived a long life, and stayed in Ephesus until death (towards the end of the 1st century). He also wrote his Bible here.

According to the council reports of the year 431, Virgin Mary stayed for a brief period in an edifice which is today replaced by the Council Church. The council meeting took place in the only church on the world dedicated to the Virgin.

St. John hid Virgin Mary in a house, which he built among

Fountains of holy water of Virgin Mary.

House of Virgin Mary and statues of Virgin Mary.

dense forests on the skirts of Bülbül Mountain. The Virgin led a humble and tranquil life here. It is believed that Virgin Mary stayed at the house on the Bülbül Mountain, and died here. After Christianity was spread, a church was built in the location where Virgin Mary spent her final days. The Christian population living around Ephesus continued the tradition of their ancestors until the end of 18th century, and held commemo-

rating ceremonies at this house every year on August 15. The place was later left in oblivion, and turned into ruins.

Catherine Emmerich (1774-1824), a physically-disabled German nun, described the location of the House of the Virgin Mary which she saw in her dreams. Emmerich also claimed that she saw in her dereams the tortures against the Christians, the arrival of Virgin Mary and St.John in Ephesus, giving de-

tailed information that the house is located on a mountain in the vicinity of Ephesus, and even furter detail on the house. This disabled woman depicted the area in great detail although she never visited it. Therefore, the priest Eugene Poulin, the Director of İzmir College, sent a delegate to Ephesus in 1891 to see whether the pious nun was telling the truth. The long researches conducted on the mountains on the north of Ephesus revealed the sacred location called the "Panhagia Kapulu". After the first expedition, Poulin travelled to Ephesus to see the place. He developed his research with scientific findings. Monseigneur Timoti, the archbishop of İzmir, showed serious interest in the House of Virgin Mary in Ephesus.

Later, many theologists agreed that the place was real. In 1892, Monseigneur Timoti allowed religious ceremonies here. Pope Jean 23 ended the discussion over the House of Virgin Mary, and declared it a spot for pilgrimage. In 1867 Pope Paul 6, in 1979 Pope John Paul 1, and on 26 November 2006 Pope Benedictus 16 visisted the place.

The house of Virgin Mary is located on a road which liead from Magnesium gate of Ephasus to the Bülbül Mountain (420 meters). It is at a distance of 8 kilometers to the ancient city. The first findings were a small, round cistern, located on the small square at a distance of 100 meters to the house, and the walls with niches on the hillside of the cistern. The stairs of the cistern, which was built for animals, have been destroyed. The excavations conducted around the wall revealed graves which were oriented towards the house. One of the two coins that were found was dated back to the reign of Emperor Constantine, and the other to the reign of Emperor Justinian.

The path extending beyond the cistern leads to the House of Virgin Mary. The house has a crucifix plan, and looks like a small church with a dome. Its well-preserved walls are dated back to 6th or 7th century. When the house was discovered, it lacked a roof, and the walls were deteriorated. Sister Marie de Mandat Grancer purchased the land, and repaired the house and arranged the surrounding area with her own sources. The original form of the house was retained, and it was covered with a roof of glass. The architect Raymond Pere built an altar of marble inside the church. During later repairs, the new walls and the ancient walls were separated by a red line.

The entrance to the house is through a narrow, vaulted door. The narrow narthex leads to the main interior. The bronze stat-

Oblations in the vicinity of the House of Virgin Mary.

Cistern near the House of Virgin Mary.

ue of Virgin Mary in the apsis was planted there after the edifice was discovered. There are niches for various purposes on both sides of the apsis. The part which is distinguished from the gray floor marble is estimated to be the hearthstone. The coals found here were dated through analyses, and it was confirmed that they were used during the time when Virgin Mary lived. The room on the right is known as the bedroom of Virgin Mary. Since the remains of another room, which should be on the left according to the plan, could not be found, the place was closed during repairs.

The waters from the spring right behind the house flows through the fountains in the terrace located below the house. This spring is believed to be sacred and healing. Believers traveling from all around the world worship here and present offerings.

Declared on of the most sacred places on earth by the Vatican, the House of Virgin Mary is a holy place visited by Christians from all around the world. Every year on August 15th, on the anniversary of ascension of Virgin Mary, sermons are held at the house.

THE VILLAGE OF SİRİNCE

Situated at 9 km east of Selçuk, the village of Sirince spreads on the mountain, showing a good example of Ottoman architecture with its narrow streets and its handsome provincial houses dating back to the XIXth century. Its first foundation is believed to date back to 14th century, when a large population of Christians coming from Ephesus settled there. Dido Sotiriu, in his book "My Greetings to Anatolia", mentions that village.

There are two churches. The one standing at the entrance to the village is made of wood. There is no inscription as for its dedication. The narthex on the western side is completely destroyed. Its lateral walls have a row of windows in between which are the frescoes of the 12 Apostles.

The second church situated on the east of the village is dedicated to St. John the Baptist. An inscription over the door mentions the restoration in 1805. It is a church from the XVII century with three naves with columns and is covered by two domes supported by vaults. Thanks to the restoration led by the administration of the Ephesus Museum, the church has been rebuilt from its ruins.

Şirince Village.

Interior of the Ephesus Archaeological Museum.

THE EPHESUS MUSEUM

The remains brought to the surface during the excavations of the site of Ephesus that lasted more than one century were sent first to England, and then to Vienna. Since 1929, they have been gathered in the local Ephesus Museum where they are exhibited in seven rooms according to the locations where they were found.

Room of the Residential Quarter

Here are , in chronological order, the artefacts and architectural items found in the residential quarter of the city. The Houses of the Slope, which have been systematically excavated since 1950. According to ancient written sources, the quarter, built on a necropolis of the 1st century B.C., containe the most beautiful examples of Roman houses of the period.

In the middle of the room, there are two round marble tables used as the altar, which evidence that religious ceremonies were held in the houses. The top of the tables are decorated with a game of backgammon, which must be engraved in a later period because it was very popular game for the Romans. Many examples of that type have been found in Ephesus. Furthermore, a table and a bronze stool, taps decorated by personages which ornamented the fountains of the houses, the most common motif being Eros riding on a dolphin, and finally a marble bath are exhibited.

To the left, in a show-case, are the surgical instruments which belonged to the famous Ephesian doctors Rufus and Soranos, accompanied by some notes

Statue of Eros on a bronze dolphin.

about their use and for which type of treatment they were employed. On the narrow wall, a fresco represents the portrait of the famous philosopher Socrates. Then comes a representation of a life-size reclining man, drinking wine, while a servant lights a oil lamp. The feet of the couch and of the lamp are original. On the large wall, one can see statues of the gods Bes and Priapus with indications about their cult.

Room of the Fountains

In this room are the statues which decorated the nymphaea (monumental fountain) of Ephesus. On the left, in a niche, we see the group called "Polyphemes" which has for its theme the adventures of Ulysses when he returns from the Trojan War, as told in Homer's Odyssey. The frieze relates the fight of Ulysses against the Cyclops Phemus, son of Poseidon, who fed on human flesh. "Ulysses and his compagnons, captured in the island of Polyphemus, managed to free themselves by piercing his only

Statue of resting warrior.

Copy of pediment of the Temple of Isis. Odysseus Polifemo group, 1st century B.C.

eye with a sharp stake, after he became intoxicated with wine". That frieze, which decorated the pediment of the Temple of Isis on the administrative agora, was transferred to the Fountain of Pollio on Dominitian Square.

Across, one can notice a group of statues which decorated the Fountain of Trajan, representing Dionysius, a satyr, Aphrodite, the Emperor Trajan and the members of the imperial family. On the wall is a sketch which shows the exact emplacement of the statues on the monument.

In the middle of the room is exhibited the statue of the "Resting Warrior" found on a pedi-ment of a fountain, showing a reclining, half naked soldier, leaning on his shield. On the other side are statues of nymphs and tritons which ornamented two storeys of the Nympheum of Laeceanus Bassus which stood in the south east corner of the administrative agora.

The Garden

Here the capitals (of the columns) are exhibited in a chronological order, from the Archaic Period to the Selcuks. We will notice the reconstruction of the pediment of the Temple of Isis with the frieze "Polypemes" whose statues are all copies.

In the west corner stand the sarcophagus of the Muses decorated with reliefs. According to the lid inscription, it was used by 2 different persons. The second sarcophagus belong to the monumental tomb of Belevi (12 km on the Selçuk-Izmir road) which is claimed to be the Tomb of Antiochos II. It is a small replica of the famous Mausoleum

Head of Lysimakhos.

of Halicarnassus, considered as one of the Seven Wonders of the World.

Room of the Sarcophagi

Though the necropolis of Ephesus has not yet been excavated, the collection of the museum presents many sarcophagi and funerary artefacts.

At the entrance, on the right, we can notice many examples of Anatolian tombs; in the first showcase is a Mycenean tomb which was found during the lay out of the parking area near the basilica of St. John. The second showcase exhibits ceramic objects found in tombs which are dated back to the Archaic Period until the Byzantine Era. On the floor is a sarcophagus from the Archaic Period brought up to light during the excavations of the commercial agora. That type of sarcophagus in terra cotta was discovered for the first time in Clazomenes (near Urla), hence its name "sarcophagus of Clazomenes", because its presents a sumptuous decoration like those executed in Clazomenes. The present one shows a lid decorated with red geometrical motifs. In this room, we can also see urns and a small sarcophagus found in the Grotto of the Seven Sleepers.

The end of the room is reserved to the cult of Cybele, the mother goddess of Asia Minor whose story is explained. It is told that the most ancient statue in terra cotta of Cybele is the one discovered in the excavations of the tumulus of Catalhöyük (Konya), dating back to the 7th century B.C., with its heavy breast symbolizing abundance and fertility, and a small statue found in Hacilar (Burdur) from the 6th century B.C. They represent the oldest statues of the world of the Neolithic Period. The cult of Cybele, mother goddess of the Hittites was perpetuated in Asia Minor until the end of the Roman period. We will notice here a statue of Cybele holding a tambourine in her hand, with Attis and Zeuso on each side.

Room of the Artemision

The room hosts all the statues of the goddess Artemis found in Ephesus, as well as fragments belonging to the Artemision.

During antiquity, the cult dedicated to the goddess Artemis was followed until the 1st century A.D., the beginning of Christianity. Her cult spread over an extensive territory. Statues or relieves of the goddess were found in Cyprus, in the south of France, in Central Europe and in all of Asia Minor. The tradition of making precious offerings to assure the realization of wishes continued for centuries. Among the objects offered were artefacts in gold, silver, electrum and ivory, some of which are exhibited in a showroom.

The most important objects of the Efes Museum are two statues of Artemis which are exhibited in this room. The statue standing on the left of the entrance is the "Great Artemis", the other is the "Beautiful Artemis".

The "Great Artemis, dated back to the 1st century A.D. reflects the Asian influence of Cybele. She hold a lion on each arm, her straight legs are touching each other, while her extended hand offers abundance. Her head, wearing a tiara (polo) made of three rows resembling the facade of a temple, is adorned on each side by five lions, bulls and griffins. The lines of her face are haughty and her large eyes seem fixed on the future. Her breasts in four rows have the form of eggs. At the beginning, it was thought to be a symbol of the nourishing breasts, but later on, it was recognized to be the symbol of the testicles of bulls sacrificed in her name. Her waist is girt by a band with rosettes and bees, the emblem of the city of Ephesus. The narrow skirt is divided in square on which are represented lions, panthers, rams and griffins.

The "Beautiful Artemis" is made of fine marble. The re-

Zeus the God.

markable differences from the first statue are the zodiac signs designed on the chest and the deer placed on each side. According to the traces left around the neck, it is probable that the statue was originally plated with gold leaves.

Room of the Cult of the Emperors

The statue standing on the right of the room, is the statue of Stephonos, a Consul of Ephesus. He holds a handkerchief in his hand, the arm extended as if giving the start of a play or a race; in the other hand he holds a crosier. To the left one can admire the friezes of the Temple of Hadrian: the foundation of Ephesus and the procession of Dionysus. During the temple's restoration, those friezes were replaced by their copies. We can also see the altar that was standing in front of the Temple of Domitian. Covered with relieves, the narrow side represents the sacrifice of a bull, and the larger side, the weapons.

Right in front of the altar are the arm and the head of the Emperor Domitian, fragments that belonged to a colossal statue of 7 meters high. Walking towards the exit of the room, on the narrow wall, we will notice the friezes which were on the Monument of Parthes, standing in Celsius Library.

The Turkish Bath and the Covered Bazaar (Arasta)

The Turkish Bath of Saadet Hatun, date back to the 15th century and standing at the southern extremity of the museum, has been restored in order to exhibit artefacts belonging to that type of building. The origin of the Turkish baths (hamam) goes back to the on the Roman Baths which were not only a place where people washed, but also got a massage, rested while making conversations with each other and exercising. For the Romans, the baths held an important place in the tradition which continued until the middle of the Byzantine period. Later, it was forgotten in the Mediterranean countries and in the west. Selcuks and Ottomans built many magnificent baths in all over Anatolia.

For the Turks, the covered bazaar was a commercial area bringing together craftsmen corporations in narrow streets (Arasta Bazaar). The Covered Bazaar of the Ephesus Museum brought some of them together, including the millwrights, reed braiders, hairdressers, copper craftsmen, sellers of glass trinkets and of rose essence.

Head of a commander.

Kuşadasi

KUŞADASI

One of the most important touristic centers of Turkey was Kuşadası on the Aegean coast. Besides, it is the accommodation and entertainment center for the tourists who travel to visit historical sites such as Ephesus, Priene, Miletus and Didim. The shelter for ships, Kuşadası has many modern hotels. Its proximity to rich, historical sites of Turkey and its 20 kilometer-long beaches made it one of the most important centers four tourism in Turkey.

Known as Neopolis in the ancient era, the area was founded in Yılancı Burnu, near the city center. It was one of the major harbors of Anatolia that lead to the Mediterranean. The remains of ancient cities are still visible underwater. Entering the Ottoman rule in 1413, the site is named the Kuşadası (Island of Birds), after the Pigeon Island which hosts the nests of birds.In the 17th century, Öküz Mehmet Paşa surrounde Kuşadası with walls. Today, only the Kale Kapısı has survived.

Öküz Mehmet Paşa Camii and its caravanserai, which were also built by the same pasha in 1618 are also among the most important historical edifices in Kuşadası. The caravanserai, built on two storeys around an interior courtyard, containst 56 rooms, and operated as a hotel today.

Connected to the mainland by a breakwater, the Pigeon Island used to be an important military base for the area. The fortress, which was built in the Byzantine era, was restored in 1834. The illuminated fortress has become a place for resting and entertainment.